Dear Parent:

Congratulations! Your child is taking
the first steps on an exciting journey.
The destination? Independent reading!

STEP INTO READING® will help your child get there. The program offers
five steps to reading success. Each step includes fun stories and colorful art.
There are also Step into Reading Sticker Books, Step into Reading Math
Readers, Step into Reading Phonics Readers, Step into Reading Write-In
Readers, and Step into Reading Phonics Boxed Sets—a complete literacy
program with something to interest every child.

Learning to Read, Step by Step!

Ready to Read   Preschool–Kindergarten
• big type and easy words • rhyme and rhythm • picture clues
For children who know the alphabet and are eager to
begin reading.

Reading with Help   Preschool–Grade 1
• basic vocabulary • short sentences • simple stories
For children who recognize familiar words and sound out
new words with help.

Reading on Your Own   Grades 1–3
• engaging characters • easy-to-follow plots • popular topics
For children who are ready to read on their own.

Reading Paragraphs   Grades 2–3
• challenging vocabulary • short paragraphs • exciting stories
For newly independent readers who read simple sentences
with confidence.

Ready for Chapters   Grades 2–4
• chapters • longer paragraphs • full-color art
For children who want to take the plunge into chapter books
but still like colorful pictures.

STEP INTO READING® is designed to give every child a successful
reading experience. The grade levels are only guides. Children can progress
through the steps at their own speed, developing confidence in their
reading, no matter what their grade.

Remember, a lifetime love of reading starts with a single step!

Step into Reading, Random House, and the Random House colophon are registered trademarks of Random House, Inc.

Visit us on the Web!
StepIntoReading.com
Seussville.com

Educators and librarians, for a variety of teaching tools, visit us at randomhouse.com/teachers

Library of Congress Cataloging-in-Publication Data
Rabe, Tish.
How to help the Earth / by the Lorax with Tish Rabe ; illustrated by Christopher Moroney and Jan Gerardi. — 1st ed.
    p. cm. — (Step into reading. Step 3)
ISBN 978-0-375-86977-8 (pbk.) — ISBN 978-0-375-96977-5 (lib. bdg.)
1. Refuse and refuse disposal—Juvenile literature. 2. Recycling (Waste, etc.)—Juvenile literature.
I. Moroney, Christopher, ill. II. Gerardi, Jan, ill. III. Title.
TD792.R33 2012 333.72—dc22 2010051124

Printed in the United States of America

10 9 8 7 6 5 4 3 2 1

STEP INTO READING®   STEP 3

How to Help the Earth— by the LORAX

with Tish Rabe
illustrated by Christopher Moroney
and Jan Gerardi

Random House 🏠 New York

Hello! I'm the Lorax.
I speak for the trees
and the fish and the birds,
and I'm asking you please
to help out the earth.
I am counting on you.
Together, I know
there's a lot we can do.

First, I have a question
and I need to ask it.
Do you know where the trash goes
that's in your wastebasket?

It goes out to the curb.

Then a dump truck comes by,

heaped with big piles of trash

that are smelly and high.

Some days after that
these big piles of trash will
be buried or dumped
in a giant landfill.

Some of the garbage
that's dumped there will rot,
but most of the garbage
that's dumped there will not.

Some cities burn trash, but this trash solution creates lots of smoke, which creates air pollution.

The good news? Things don't
have to go on this way.
We can reduce trash.
We can start right away.

Take your lunch in a bag,
but don't throw it away.
Use the bag or a lunch box
again the next day.

Use both sides of your paper,

and I have no doubt

there will be much less paper

for you to throw out.

When you've read magazines
and you no longer need them,
pass them to your friends
so they'll get to read them!

Rather than tossing
your old clothes, toys, and shoes,
donate them. They're things
other people can use.

Put used soda cans in
a recycling bin.
Rinse them out when they're empty
and throw them right in!

They'll be made into new cans.
This can I have here
is made from old cans
I recycled last year.

Paper clips, rubber bands,
buttons, and screws
are things you will find
that are easy to reuse.

Put these things in a drawer
so they're all in one place.
They'll be easy to find and
won't take up much space.

23

When dead batteries are dumped,
this fact I have found:
the chemicals in them
leak into the ground.

Use rechargeable batteries.

Charge them and then

when they run out of power,

just charge them again.

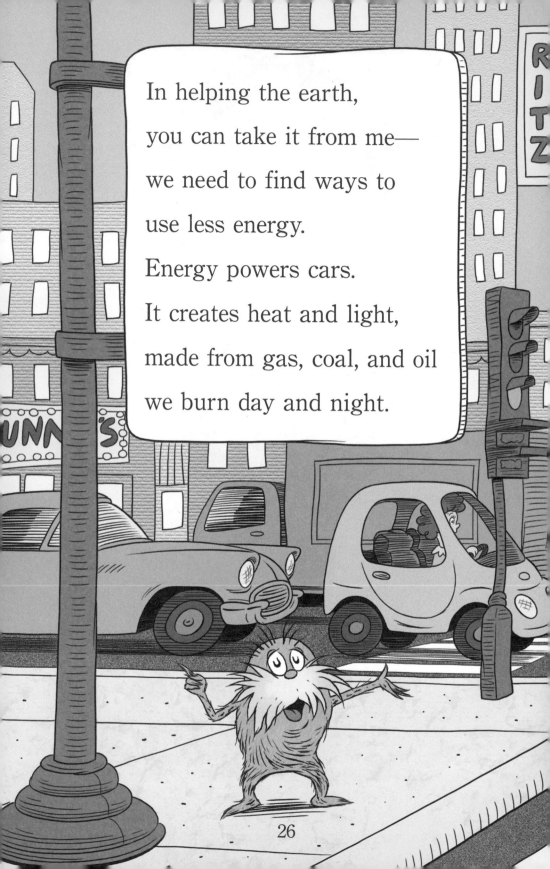

In helping the earth,
you can take it from me—
we need to find ways to
use less energy.
Energy powers cars.
It creates heat and light,
made from gas, coal, and oil
we burn day and night.

These are natural resources,
and there is a limit
to how much of them
our whole earth has within it.

We need to use less,
and I just have to say
there are ways to use less
energy every day.

When you leave a room,

stop and turn off the light.

Be sure to turn off

your computer at night.

When it's cold, wear a sweatshirt
and take the time, please,
to turn down the heat
just a couple degrees.

When you're doing your homework
or starting to read,
sunlight through a window
may be all that you need.

Animals and plants—
all things alive—
need to have water.
It's how we survive.

So water is something
we need to save, too.
There are ways we can save it.
I'll show you a few.

When you get up each morning

and stand at the sink

and start brushing your teeth,

take a moment to think.

A lot of clean water

is going to waste

while you reach for your toothbrush

and squeeze on toothpaste.

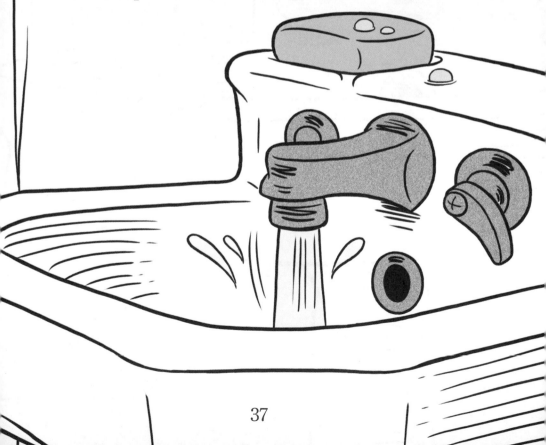

Right down the drain
this clean water is going.
So turn off the faucet
and stop it from flowing!

Spend less time in the shower
and you'll still get clean.
Try a four-minute shower.
You'll see what I mean.

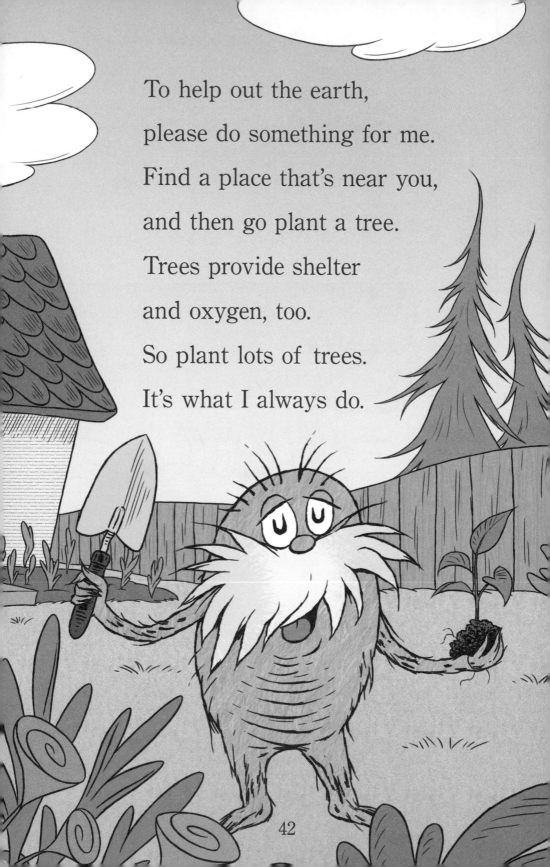

To help out the earth,
please do something for me.
Find a place that's near you,
and then go plant a tree.
Trees provide shelter
and oxygen, too.
So plant lots of trees.
It's what I always do.

If we work together,

the earth will get better.

The land will be clearer.

The soil will be wetter.

The sun will shine brighter.

The trees will be greener.

The sky will be bluer.

The air will be cleaner.

And next time I speak
for the trees, fish, and birds,
I know in my heart
I'll need only two words.

For all that you've done
and for all you will do,
I'm the Lorax, and I say a
great big . . .

. . . thank you!